# THE FUNSTEN NUT STRIKE

## Mayor Addressing Striking Nut Pickers at City Hall

# MAYOR'S GROUP
# TAKES UP STRIKE
# OF NUT PICKERS

Committee Hears Delegation of Workers, and Officers and Attorney of R. E. Funsten Co.

Mayor Dickmann and members
a committee appointed by him
t week to investigate the strike
of pickers at the R. E. Funsten
met today at City Hall to hear
evances f workers and an
a sol of the situation by mem-
s of the firm and their attor-

he strikers sent a committee of
men who insisted that Wil-
m Sentner rejected as a
presentative of the group ac-
mpany them. Jacob M Lashley,
ney for the company, said the
mittee Sentner was a Com

Photo and caption from May 23, 1933 St. Louis *Post-Dispatch*. The Mayor (arrow) is addressing the strikers.

# THE FUNSTEN NUT STRIKE

**Myrna Fichtenbaum**

International Publishers, New York

## DEDICATION

*To Leo whose love and enduring support made this possible.*
*To our children — Rudy, Heidi and Carl — whose openness to new*
*ideas speaks of a younger generation whose will can impose a more*
*humane world.*

© 1991 International Publishers Co., Inc.

First Printing 1992

Manufactured in the United States of America

Library of Congress Cataloging-in-Publication Data

Fichtenbaum, Myrna
    The Funsten Nut strike / Myrna Fichtenbaum.
        p.    cm.
    Includes bibliographical references (p.          ) and index.
    ISBN 0-7178-0696-0 (pbk.) : $4.50
    1. Funsten Nut Company Strike, Saint Louis, Mo., 1933  I. Title.
HD5325.N862 1933.S25   1991
331.89'2864804520977865—dc 20                          91-29487
                                                           CIP

# PREFACE

The following account of a group of working women, in particular African American women, was written in 1973. The original introduction (p. xi) sought to outline in a small way the relevant social fabric of that time in an effort to link it, in part, with the social forces that interacted during the period of the Funsten Nut strike, i.e., 1933.

Continuous perseverance in the struggle for equality and justice have resulted in important changes since this account was written. One of the most significant social changes that has occurred has been the catapulting of women into the workforce on a scale not seen before. Women represent 46% of the current workforce and it is predicted that in the year 2,000, two out of every three entrants into the workforce will be females and minorities.

However, despite their escalating numbers, women largely remain in lower paying jobs. The struggle to move out of these to more desirable wage and decision-making jobs is still to be accomplished. Another change that has occurred is that the wages of African

American and white women are presently almost equal if we take into account regional differences. On the other hand, while women now earn an average of 69% of men's wages, the gap remains large.

Union organization continues to be an instrument to eradicate inequity. Whereas this was a phenomenon on the rise in the 1930s, it has been more sporadic in 1980s and the 1990s. The need to organize working women into militant, rank-and-file led unions remains an essential but unfinished task of the labor movement, the women's movement and the civil rights movement.

The 1980s and 1990s under Reagan and Bush have ushered in an era of greater inequity, despite the few individual exceptions. Affirmative action plans, comparable wage rates and the efforts to eradicate sexual and racial discrimination have been diluted by Supreme Court decisions.

There has been a resurrection of women working in the home. A new phenomenon is the increasing number of women in part-time jobs without benefits and health care coverage.

Increasing numbers of women entering the workforce bring more dramatically into focus the shortage of affordable, quality daycare.

The concepts of the pauperization of women and the feminization of poverty emerging during this recent period reflects the deterioration of the general living conditions among women.

More recently however, the militant, inspirational struggle of African American women in the Mississippi catfish industry is perhaps a hallmark of events yet to come.

This successful struggle for unionization reminds us that victories can be won even in the most trying times. The determination of this group of women to achieve dignity and a better life represents one link between the present and the past as it unfolds in the following account.

*Myrna Fichtenbaum*

Demonstration down Market Street, 1932. Note that slogans include "Free Scottsboro Boys" as well as calls for use of funds for city relief.

# CONTENTS

*Illustrations: Frontispiece, viii, x, p. 2*
*Used with permission from the Western Historical Manuscript*
*Collection, University of Missouri–St. Louis*

Unemployed demonstration with St. Louis city hall in background.

# INTRODUCTION

The struggles of Black people and the participation of women in the fabric of American life have suffered from scholarly neglect and racist attitudes. Little has been recorded of the role in American history that women generally, and Black women, in particular, have played in the shaping of the American tradition. The denial of a history is a cornerstone of a lack of humanity and an important principle in the maintenance of an inferior position. In the 1920s, referring to women and history, Professor Arthur M. Schlesinger said: "An examination of the standard histories of the United States and of the history text books in our schools raises the pertinent question whether women have ever made any contributions to American national progress that are worthy of record. If the silence of the historians is to mean anything, it would appear that one half of our population have been negligible factors in our country's history..."[1] On the omissions of historiography, Dr. W.E.B. Dubois wrote, "We have the record of kings and gentlemen ad nauseum and in stupid detail, but of the common run of human beings, and particularly of the half or wholly submerged working group, the world has saved all too little of authentic record and tried to forget or ignore even the little saved. With regard to Negroes in America ... came also the attempt, conscious or unconscious, to excuse the shame of slavery by stressing natural inferiority which would render it impossible for Negroes to make, much less leave, any record of revolt or struggle, any human reaction to utter degradation."[2]

It is the "common run of human beings" by whom history is made, for where would our glorious heroes have been without those many who made their visions and plans a reality? And further, from where would those heroes have arisen if not from the social conditions, engulfing the "common run of human beings," which required their leadership. It is the ordinary laboring folk, the makers of history, but more particularly, about women laborers, that this account is concerned.

With a determination and insistence that the voice of women will be heard in their own behalf, a movement has emerged whose goal is to achieve broader rights and opportunities for one-half of the population to whom these rights have thus far been denied.

Across the country during 1973, we witnessed several conferences of working women within the trade union movement. In St. Louis, a conference of both union and non-union women was held in November, sponsored by the St. Louis Women's Labor Coalition. Its major objective was to unite the energies of working women in factories, stores, and offices to improve their conditions. Its emphasis was twofold: that of organization of unorganized working women into trade unions as a means of achieving their economic, social and political goals and, to encourage women to assume representation on all levels of union leadership. Viewed in the context of achieving increased benefits for all working people, its statement of purpose said. "... in fighting discrimination on the job and by joining together for improved working conditions and more equitable pay...by encouraging women to assume positions of leadership in the labor movement ... women will make the trade union movement stronger and help to improve conditions for all workers."

In March of 1974, the first national conference of the Coalition of Labor Union

Women was held in Chicago. The voice of 3,500 women was heard as one when its statement of purpose was adopted asserting that "... we take aggressive steps to more effectively address ourselves to the critical needs of 30 million unorganized sisters and to make our unions more responsive to the needs of all women, especially needs of minority women, who have been singled out for blatant discrimination. Full equality of opportunities and rights in the labor force require the full attention of the labor movement ... especially, the full attention of women who are part of the labor movement."

The civil rights struggles of the 1960s, focusing on the inequality of Black Americans, gave birth to what has been referred to as the "women's liberation movement." Not uncommonly, broad movements for social change focusing on one kind of injustice make fertile the soil from which sprout a variety of seedlings whose roots branch out, strangling other forms of injustice.

By the early 1920s, it was widely believed that opposition to the inequality of women was the concern of only a small segment of middle class and professional women. The emergence of the Coalition of Labor Union Women (CLUW) within the organized labor movement is testimony to the notion that working-class women are also not satisfied with their condition of inequality. Thus the struggle to alter the status of American working women is not simply tied to the efforts of a small group of female individuals, but is closely connected with the major social forces of our time which seek to transform our urbanized, industrial society by increasing political participation, by challenging the present distribution of wealth, by questioning traditional roles, and most of all, by scrutinizing the extent of human equality.

Within the struggles of these social forces, women play an important role and, in particular, Black women, because of their triple oppression, by race and sex and as workers, have been a pivotal force.

To understand current social movements, it is valuable to explore their historical antecedents. In so doing, we establish the historical continuity which links the past with the present. It also provides insight into the extent of growth and level of maturity, over time, exhibited by those forces spearheading change. This account records a piece of women's history, thereby assisting future efforts to more fully evaluate our history.

In time of great upheaval, injustice seems more intolerable. It is, perhaps, the dialectical interconnection between hopelessness and hope attaining a heightened level of fragility which accounts for the organization of women advancing the struggle for women's rights. With unprecedented inflation, a high rate of unemployment, an energy crisis and a loss of confidence in the present political leadership, present-day crises [1973] are reminiscent in some respects of the upheaval of the 1930s. What were some of the crucial factors affecting women which characterized that earlier period of time?

A sizable number of women acting as a group in St. Louis, Missouri, sought to change the conditions under which they labored and thus change, somewhat, the quality of their lives. It is of further interest because the predominant number of women involved, and their leaders, were Black. This fact adds significance to their struggle. Black women have always been more sensitive to and more hampered by racial oppression than sexual oppression. Nevertheless, the two have always complemented one another.

In the current struggle for women's full equality, it is important to see the connection between those two social currents. The struggle described in this paper combines these with the larger struggles of labor in its efforts for human dignity.

The scope of this account is limited to the issues, problems, personalities and outcome of the specific incident under investigation, namely, the Funsten Nut Strike in August of 1933.

The research included reading the newspaper articles written at the time about the incident. We also attempted to locate union publications. In addition, a limited search was made for the papers of some of the members of the Citizen's Committee who played a role. Unfortunately, the papers of Mayor Dickman were not located, and those of one of the members of the Citizen's Committee didi not contain any direct reference to the Funsten Strike.

A former, long-time, recently retired worker of the Provident Association, Mrs. Elmer Moisee, was interviewed, as was a retired, elderly, former employee of the Urban League, Mrs. J. Buckner—both of whom recalled the times and the strike.

An effort was made to locate former workers at the factory who had been employed there during the strike. This was done in two ways. Through the kind inquiring efforts of friends, coworkers and activists and in addition, the aid of the administrator at two predominantly white senior citizen centers was enlisted. Several of those interviewed had worked at Funsten before the strike occurred and had left prior to its happening. Only four of all those interviewed actually worked there during the strike. None of those interviewed were in the leadership, or were members of the committees, or in any way partook in any of the activities involved relating to the strike, with the exception of one woman who recalled having attended a few of the general meetings called by the strike committee. All of those interviewed were Black except for one white woman.

A lengthy letter was sent to the wife of the union organizer, now deceased, William Sentner, who was in the leadership of the strike. Unfortunately, his papers were not located. However, Mrs. Antonia Sentner, having also been a Communist and actively involved in community affairs, was helpful in her extensive reply in attempting to give a picture of the times, as well as anything she did recall about the strike and the personalities involved. In, addition, Ralph Shaw, the leader of the Communist Party of St. Louis during that time, now residing in another city, was interviewed.

Finally, an appointed official of the city government, David Grant, whose association with the city began at the time and who was himself involved in an aspect of the incident under study, was also interviewed. In addition, a conversation was held with the then chief executive of the nut company, Mr. Hugh L. King, who had been with the firm for many years.

The labor movement in St. Louis was very much in flux during the period under study and local labor publications that were sought appear to have been discontinued for a period of time.

As in the case of all historical research, many documents were, unfortunately, not preserved and it is with much elation that one observes a changed attitude developing, with a greater sensitivity towards the need to preserve not only the letters and documents of famous men and women, but also of various groups, particularly those hitherto ignored.

The only written, original documents uncovered were two leaflets written by those in leadership of the strike (see Appendix).

# THE FUNSTEN NUT STRIKE

Headquarters of the Communist Party on 1948 Garrison Ave, St. Louis.

# WOMEN IN THE WORKFORCE, 1930

According to the census of 1930, there were 49,000,000 gainfully employed workers; women accounted for 22% of this national workforce. Percentagewise, Black women accounted for twice as many of those employed as compared to white working women.[3]

By far the largest percentage of women, nearly 30%, were employed in domestic and personal service. This included jobs in hotels, restaurants, beauty parlors, or in private homes as cooks, chambermaids, cleaning women, maids, laundresses, etc. A sizable increase of women in clerical positions established it as the second largest category of female employment in 1930. The third largest category was in manufacturing and mechanical industries. This category appears to have been effected by certain shifts in subdivisions. While there was a decline in the independent sewing trades, there was an increase in those employed in clothing factories. Black women, however, were discriminated against in hiring policies on these jobs. Among the industries that saw an increase in women workers over a ten-year period, were the food and allied industries. Black women outnumbered white in agriculture and represented more than a third of the women employed in domestic service.[4]

Not differing too much from present-day conditions, women received less pay than men for the same jobs. Over an eleven year period, by 1932, women's earnings in women-employed industries averaged from 45 to 84% of men's. It is interesting to learn that with the passage of NRA codes in 1933, sex differential in wages was recognized and institutionalized by the federal government. According to a statement issued by the Women's Bureau in 1934, "not far from a fourth of the codes" adopted a lower rate for women workers. Also very much in accord with the present-day wage scales, just as women earned less than men, Black women earned less than white women. As an example, in cigar and cigarette factories where Black women in the south were sizably employed, the median income was $10.10 for Black women in 1930, as compared with $16.30 per week for white women.[5]

Exact figures of unemployment for women during that time were not known. However, the Women's Bureau estimated that there were two million women unemployed, while

4

Grace Hutchins, in her book *Women Who Work*, estimated female unemployment at four million. In all age groups up to thirty years of age, larger proportions of women than men were without jobs, because married men labeled as "heads of household" — were largely given job preference. In her 1933 annual report, Mary Anderson, chief of the U.S. Women's Bureau, stated that unemployment was more widespread among young women workers than among young men workers, and increasing at a more rapid rate. Dismissal rates among married women workers increased as well.[6]

The high jobless rate was, of course, responsible for enormous demands for relief. Generally, single women were denied relief since there were not sufficient funds available. Evictions were common and homelessness was a sufficient reality to establish it as a topic of discussion as well as struggle. Hutchins reports that, "Well fed members of women's clubs, meeting at the Hotel Astor, New York City, in May, 1933, listened to a vivid description of how 75,000 homeless girls and women spend their days and nights. "If you know how to go uptown, downtown, and across town, you can ride all night for a nickel." The number of families on relief in major cities was 85% to 90% more in August of 1933 than in the same month of 1932.[7]

In Missouri, in 1930, women represented 30% of the workforce.[8] In St. Louis, there were 386,000 gainfully employed workers, 27.4% of whom were women,[9] 11.4% in St. Louis were Black residents and slightly more than half of those were women.[10]

While occupations for Black workers in St. Louis generally were limited, they were particularly so for Black women. Occupations open to Black women were hairdresser, waitress, cafeteria help, seamstress, housework, laundry, tobacco factory and nut factory. The chief alternatives were in laundry for $2.00 or $2.50 per washing or irregular maid or housework at practically the same rate.[11]

During the depression there was a great decrease in the rate of wages and of course this applied to women workers. The general tendency on the part of many manufacturers was to cut wages, lengthen hours and fail to meet employment requirements for industrial safety and sanitation.

A common way for employers to avoid the overhead costs incurred with the establishment of workplaces and factories and maintain wages at their lowest possible rate was the institution of industrial home work.

6

"The exploitation of women doing industrial home work has been especially appalling. While fourteen states (1933) have laws that limit the evils of industrial home work, the practice has increased with the general breaking down of employment standards in the recent years of the depression. More and more employers are unable or unwilling to meet the overhead expenses necessary to operate a factory, and are giving the work out to be done at home at shockingly low wages."[12]

One industry in St. Louis which had relatively large numbers of women in its employ was the men's clothing industry. In particular, the ready-made clothing houses employed large numbers of women both in less skilled and in many highly skilled processes. In 1930, of 11,699 gainful workers who were employed in the St. Louis clothing industries, 7,283 were women. This industry took advantage of the depression by introducing piece work, and reduced pay rates to low levels.[13]

During this period, women employed locally in the meatpacking industry were earning $.29 per hour and working ten hours a day despite the fact that Missouri was one of the fourteen states providing for a nine-hour day. Discussing violations in her 1931 report,

Commissioner Amanda Hargis reported, "I find there is a tendency to violate the nine hour law in Missouri in industry more than any other industrial law."[14] In a 1933 publication of the Women's Bureau, it was noted, "During the present period of unemployment no standards have been secure. Even when upheld through legislation or by strong trade union organization, serious breakdowns have occurred."[15]

# BLACK WORKERS, WOMEN AND THE TRADE UNION MOVEMENT

As previously indicated, an industry in which there existed a sizable number of women was the garment industry. Among the unions which had organized in that industry was the Amalgamated Clothing Workers. However, one of its major difficulties was that the men's clothing industry was in the hands of big business enterprises that frequently were national firms, as compared to the ladies clothing industry, which was dominated by small owner shops more vulnerable to active labor demands. The development of smaller shops in this segment of the industry was due to the frequent styling changes in women's clothes in contrast to the relatively stable styles for men. Employers were eager to make use of both women's willingness to work at lower wages than men doing like work would have been willing to accept and, also, of their indifference to any concerted action and organization within the men's clothing industry.[16]

Another union organizing in ladies garments was the International Ladies Garment

Workers Union. For many years the ILGWU was faced with the problem of organizing women. "There are in St. Louis (1932) several thousand dress and skirtmakers still unorganized.... In 1920 the International made a serious attempt to organize these women but the lack of response among these workers did not warrant extending the campaign which had already proved costly and unsuccessful."[17]

Nationally, in a document of the Women's Bureau referring to unions, it was noted that, "...few unions have made any attempt to include them as organized workers. The International Ladies Garment Workers Union and the Amalgamated Clothing Workers have made an effort to include them. However, none of the unions that are open to Negroes have made much progress in organizing Negro women workers."[18]

While the numbers of women in organized labor was generally small, this was particularly true with regard to Black workers, men and women. The major obstacle was the discriminatory policies of the AFL, the major trade union organization during this period, toward Black workers. The discrimination can be discerned in several ways. Initially it pursued a policy of sanctioning unions whose charters specifically excluded Black workers. Later, in a changed position, it issued charters only to unions that did not explicitly bar Blacks in their constitutions. This permitted acts of subterfuge and the creation of segregated locals. Finally, its discriminating policies can be evidenced in its refusal to organize the numbers of unskilled workers among whom a large preponderance were Black.[19]

# RACIAL SITUATION IN ST. LOUIS – 1933

In the 1930s, St. Louis was a "jimcrow," highly segregated town and this was certainly true for local industry. In the main, Black workers, men and women, were employed only in menial jobs. The major field of employment for Black women was as domestics, but many preferred to work in the nut industry despite its very low wages.[20] Antonia Sentner recalled that when Blacks were employed on jobs where whites were also employed, they were physically separated and separate facilities were maintained for the Black workers.[21] Shops that did solicit and permit Black consumers refused to hire Black sales clerks.

Housing was restricted to specific areas of the city and walking in other residential areas was viewed with great suspicion.

There were no Black officials in any locally elected or appointed political office.

St. Louis was the last stop on the railroad before entering the South. It was here that the cars were changed to designations of "Colored" and "White."

Black people were not permitted use of public accommodations and they were confined to Black-owned eating places and movie houses.

It was a time before the existence of Homer Phillips Hospital and stricken Black patients who had to be hospitalized were housed in the basement of City Hospital.

Of course, the status of being less than human was intensified on the economic front, as indicated in a Women's Bureau publication, "The industrial depression ... has fallen with particular severity on the Negro workers. One result of the depression... is that Negro waitresses and other domestics are being displaced by white workers."[22]

In a letter to a member of the Speaker's Bureau of the Urban League requesting that he address a community group on Black problems, the executive secretary, John Clark, encouraged him to emphasize that "... approximately 75% of all working Negroes in St. Louis are either unemployed, or underemployed, consequently, undernourished, inadequately housed and clothed..."[23]

A significant form of resistance to discrimination and the burdens of the depression was the disproportionate number of Black men and women in the unemployed movements

13

of that time which sought to achieve a measure of relief. Through militant actions which achieved some successes, they transformed despair into hope. In St. Louis, Black workers were active participants within the leadership of this group as well as in its membership. Locally, the movement reached one of its most dramatic climaxes in July of 1932. An instance of this involvement was recalled by a retired Urban League field representative and placement secretary, Mrs. J. Buckner, when she said, "Mrs. Wallace, who became a day worker for the League, was one of those nut pickers and she became very militant. When the Negro women were sitting in at the City Hall and refused to leave, Mrs. Wallace's picture appeared in the *Post Dispatch* as one of the women who had spent several nights down there."[24]

# THE NUT INDUSTRY, THE FUNSTEN NUT CO.—EMPLOYEES AND THEIR WORKING CONDITIONS

For some time St. Louis was the center of the pecan industry because pecans grow naturally along the Mississippi Valley regions and could be harvested and shipped by boat to St. Louis. During the regular season, there were about sixteen factories employing some 3,000 women. (This figure probably included those involved with industrial home work.) Of these, seven were owned by R. E. Funsten Company, a $75,000 corporation.[25]

R. E. Funsten, whose progenitor was a wealthy merchant who emigrated to the colonies from Ireland,[26] was born in Virginia, educated in common and high school in Virginia, and private school, and migrated to St. Louis where he started his business in 1895.[27] It was run as a family business up until about 1902 when it was incorporated with R.E. Funsten as president. In 1933, Eugene Funsten, one of his sons, was the president.[28]

Approximately eighty-five to ninety percent of the labor force in this industry were

15

Black women, working over nine hours a day, five and a half days a week, fifty-two hours a week, starting at 6:45 AM stopping at 4:45 PM with forty-five minutes for lunch. The balance of the workers were white women, mostly of Polish extraction, who started at 7:00 AM, stopped at 4:30 PM with one hour for lunch. A small handful of men, Black and white, were also employed as foremen, weighers, crackers and dryers.[29] The men also handled the packing and shipping of the nuts. According to Funsten president Hugh L. King, today [1973] their lot is "much better."[30]

In order to prevent the nuts from shattering when cracked with a crude instrument, they were first soaked in water. Then they were dried in a special room. Pecan picking was terrible work. Most of the women workers were involved in the picking operation.[31] Mary Franklin and Lottie Johnson described the work. Seated at a table, after obtaining a 25 lb. bag of nuts, the women separated the meats from the shells with a knife. Halves were placed in one pile, broken pieces in another. The shells were also kept, so that upon completion all of it could be weighed once more, making sure that it all added up to the original 25 lbs. Black walnuts were also picked occasionally, but the separation of

16

these meats was much more difficult to accomplish.[32] The job required no special skills —just speed, dexterity and patience.

Another operation in which a segment of the white women were involved was sorting. All of the operations, except for picking, were centered in the main plant on 16th and Delmar, which also housed the main office. As recalled by Nora Diamond and Evelina Ford, the vast majority of white women worked at the Delmar Street plant, although a number of Black women pickers worked there in the basement. There were also some white women working at a smaller plant on Chouteau on the first floor while the Black women worked on the second floor.[33] Evelina Ford, commented on the different times of arrival and departure saying, "'Cause at that time colored folks and white folks didn't agree very much."[34] In addition to the plants, there were store fronts and much of the picking of nutmeats was also farmed out as home work.[35]

During two years prior to 1933, the St. Louis *Post Dispatch* reported that the women had suffered five wage cuts. [36] *Labor Unity* in August 1933, however, indicated that there had been two wage cuts.[37] All sources generally indicate that the most accurate characterization of the conditions under which the women worked was "sweatshop conditions." Bathroom facilities were of primitive nature and not kept in sanitary condition. Despite the fact that this was a food industry, Mrs. Elmer Moisee pointed out that no health standards were imposed.[38] Working with the nuts emitted a dust which precipitated coughing and many of the women concluded on their own that sweetmilk was a useful antidote to this occupational hazard. This, then, was considered a necessary industrial expense, although for some this did not always solve the problem. The nutmeats produced permanent stains, thus it was necessary to wear an apron to prevent damage to one's clothes. Mrs. Josie Moore told of being provided with an apron, payment for which was deducted at the end of the week without her consent, bringing her pay to $.50 for the week. In describing the working conditions at the plant in East St. Louis where she worked she said, "It wasn't clean. They didn't have no windows. They had big doors that just come open. (When it was cold) they fastened the doors and they'd have a little heat in there, very little. They kept the lights on all the time. Oh, it was terrible. I remember a couple of women taking sick and they told the

18

man, the boss, that they would have to go home. He said, "Well if you start that going home, you just stay there."[39] Some of the other shops were not quite as bad and, of course, the main plant was considerably better. In a comment, which included a reference to disparity, Mrs. J. Buckner said, "Another part of it was that there was a shadow of racism in it too. All the girls in the factory who did the sorting and the weighing at the Delmar plant were white girls and the salesman and the supervisors were all white, while the dirty work was parceled out in the Negro community."[40]

The majority of the women employed were middle-aged with families, and about 40% were youth.[41] Almost all found it necessary to contribute to the support of other members of their families. Several expressed the view that they were forced to leave and seek employment elsewhere since they were unable to meet their obligations on the starvation wages. All those interviewed, employees and others, with the exception of the one white woman, agreed that the wage scale was atrocious. Some of the men and the white women sorters were paid on a weekly rate of approximately $3.00. The Negro pickers were paid three cents per pound for halves and two cents for pieces. Two shops paid four cents for halves and two cents for pieces. The white pickers were getting two cents more per pound. Interviewed during the strike by the St. Louis *Star Times* about their wages, some of the women stated the following. Mrs. Smith, who had worked for Funsten for 18 years, said that the highest wage she had ever made was in 1918 when she had averaged $18 a week. In 1933, however, she had never earned more than $4.00. Mrs. Cora Lewis, who supported her mother and four children, earned an average weekly wage of about $3.00. Mrs. Ardenia Bryant, who had been working for the company for about ten years, supporting herself and her invalid husband, reported her average weekly wage was about $3.00. Miss Althea Stewart had received wages as low as $.63.[42] On the whole, Negro workers were paid on the average of $1.80 per week and white workers averaged $2.75.[43] *Labor Unity* reported that approximately sixty percent of the women were on the relief rolls.[44] Another source, the Black local paper, the St. Louis *Argus*, cited this figure at 40% in 1933.[45]

A common complaint, voiced by Mrs. Buckner and Mr. Shaw, was that of being cheated in the final weighing by some of the

Negro men who were responsible for recording the work completed in order to compute the piecework rates.[46] In discussing this, Mrs. Buckner, formerly of the Urban League, explained that, "When they took the picked nuts to the weighing table, they would take another woman with them to show what the weight was. And when they left in the evening, the ticket given them for credit was different from the ticket that was posted at the time of the weighing. At the meeting I attended, one of the church members who was one of the foremen said that he allowed the women to take the nut shells home to burn for heat... and he felt he was compensating them by letting them take the nut shells home."[47]

## ORIGINS OF THE STRIKE AND ITS DEVELOPMENT

Among the numbers of people recruited into the Communist Party from the unemployment movement was a man who had two members of his family working at the Funsten company.[48] Aware of their plight, he talked with them about the possibilities of union organization. A previously spontaneous strike at the main plant in 1927 had ended in failure. At the first meeting, which included the recent recruit and Ralph Shaw, the local leader of the Communist Party, there were three women. The next one had six, until finally they had twenty women involved. From the outset the women agreed that their conditions were bad but they felt that support for their efforts was essential. A representative of the Food Workers Industrial Union, an affiliate of the Trade Union Unity League (TUUL) was assigned to help the women organize. This initial stage of meeting in homes and recruiting, and increasing the numbers of women interested, spanned a period of a few months. With the number reaching twenty, the group began discussing demands they would present to their employer.

The women themselves decided on the following demands: an increase of wages to ten cents for halves and four cents for pieces, equal wages for Black and white, and union recognition. Mrs. Carrie Smith, the heart and soul of the strike, coined the slogan "We demand ten and four." It was then that a union shop local was established with an executive committee.

It is somewhat unclear exactly where the activities originated; however, evidence does point to the west side plant, which would have been the one located on Easton, now Martin Luther King Jr. Drive. At the west side plant the union, at the time, had one hundred members out of the two hundred employees. However, they had also succeeded in getting members from other shops.[49]

In answer to a question about leadership roles, Mrs. Mary Franklin recalled, "There were four women there (at the main plant) and when they got ready to go to the conference, they would talk to Mr. Funsten all the time."[50] The women seemed very convinced that they did not want to strike unless they

23

had to. A committee of twelve was elected and on Monday, April 24th, at 7:30 AM they walked into the office and the spokeswomen stated their demands. At the same time, it had been decided that all the others (the 100) would stop work and gather outside the office to hear the answer. In this west side plant, all the workers except seven came to support the demands. The executive agreed to take their demands up with the company and give them an answer at a later date.

The women waited three weeks for an answer and then decided to extend their organization to other factories. Two meetings were concentrated at the main plant that contained 700 white and Black women. On May 12th, fifteen women from that plant joined the union, and the women decided that any further delay might weaken their forces. On Saturday, May 13th, in the evening, an open mass meeting was called at which a vote was taken on whether to strike. The vote was yes.[51]

It was agreed that the original west end plant committee would go to the office Monday morning and demand an answer to the original demands. If accepted, all would return to work. If rejected, then all would walk out, go to the main plant and give the shop committee there the signal to walk out. On the first day, nine hundred workers walked out. On the second day, two additional Funsten shops plus two other factories, The Liberty Nut Company and The Central Pecan Company joined the strike, bringing the total to 1400 women. As in the case of all other figures, there are variations reported. *Labor Unity* said, "On the morning of the second, (day) the white women walked out in solidarity with the Negro women."[52] Indications are that this did not include *all* the white women. In an interview with a white woman worker who was a sorter, Nora Diamond stated, "I worked during the strike 'cause it didn't effect me." She attributed her disapproval of the strike to her feelings, which she expressed as follows, "because it was led by the wrong kind of people, Russians, foreigners." However, she indicated that the white pickers, who were the largest percentage of the white workers, did join the strike.[53] The St. Louis *Argus* reported that picketing of the plants was carried on by both Black and white workers.[54]

The procedure followed was not a general strike call but rather one shop after another was called out to join the strike. one woman interviewed recalled that, "When they came, they hollered for us to come out, the strike is on!," and most of the women dropped their work and went out and joined in. She, however, stayed and finished her work and then eventually hired herself out as a laundress in a private home. Since her husband was a railroad worker, she did not urgently feel the need to work. She also recalled asking Mr. Funsten, who appeared at the plant that day, what was happening. His reply was that the women were going on strike for a wage increase and that they had never asked him for any increase prior to this occasion. A St. Louis *Post Dispatch*. article reported, however, that Funsten said May 17 that the disturbance began on May Day when employees on Easton made an "indirect demand" for a wage increase.[55]

Each shop elected its own strike committee and captains for the picket line. Every morning, the shop committee met, and general strike meetings were held to inform the strikers of any developments and advise them of needed actions. Mrs. Franklin said, "I went to a couple of them meetings on Garrison. One white fella named Bill did the biggest speaking and some of the ladies in the plant. They would all get together and go and tell us to come to these places where they would be."

Picketing began every morning at 5 AM and took on the character of demonstrations around the main plant. The women brought their husbands and children and they were joined by other workers, members of the Unemployed Councils and members of the Communist Party.

In addition to the central strike committee, a negotiating committee and a relief committee were established. Approximately twelve hundred women were fed daily. Food was collected from sympathetic workers and businessmen and a truckload of food came from the Workers International Relief in Chicago.[56] Commenting on attitudes of other workers to the strike, Mr. Shaw said, during his interview, "There was tremendous support and sympathy of the labor movement for these women. The bakery workers sent down a delegation and got them second-day-old bread. They made a collection at the baker's hall. If we went elsewhere, we would have gotten the same sympathy. The clothing workers, the meat cutters and bakery workers were the closest to us."

One of the difficulties in the investigation of this strike has been to ascertain specific knowledge of the women who assumed the leadership during this struggle. Indications are that some were in their late twenties and some in their forties. They seem to have had strong family and church ties. The outstanding leader among the white women seems to have been a relatively young Polish woman, Blondie Rossen. The overall strike leader was a middle-aged, dynamic Black woman with a strong sense of determination and justice, Carrie Smith. At the original mass meeting that voted to strike, with the Bible in one hand and a brick in the other, Carrie said, "Girls, we can't lose."

"She was a beautiful person. She's the one who gave it the spirit," said Ralph Shaw.[57] During the strike she articulated the demands and the sentiment of the strikers when she declared to the St. Louis *Star Times*, "We want to be paid on the basis of ten cents a pound for half nuts and four cents a pound for pieces. This would give us an average wage of about $6.00 or $7.00 a week. We think we are entitled to live as well as other folks live, and should be entitled to a wage that will provide us with ample food and clothing."[58]

There were several instances when it was necessary for a few specific women to exert their leadership. One of these times was during a meeting at City Hall. A committee of five women, three Black and two white, together with the union organizer, William Sentner, met with the City Counselor, Senti, in the absence of the mayor, to ask the city to arbitrate the dispute.[59]

Another such time was the day following the parade and demonstration in front of city hall when the mayor came out on the steps and addressed the workers.[60] At this second meeting a committee of six strikers plus Sentner met with Mr. Funsten, his legal representative, the mayor and members of the Citizen's Committee appointed by him to investigate the dispute.[61]

Once the strike began, as part of the strategy, the women's committees went to speak at all types of organizations in the community to win support for their struggle.[62] One such instance was when two white and two Black women, accompanied by an attorney for the ACLU and a high school teacher, met with the Social Justice Commission of St. Louis at Temple Israel to ask for their assistance. At this meeting they had with them evidence of their low wages in the form of several unopened pay envelopes with wages covering four days work. Of eight that were opened, two contained a little more than $2.00 and the others about $1.50.[63]

A group also made a presentation at a local church, at which several members of the Urban League were present. Mrs. Buckner recalled, "I was a speaker at that meeting in Rev. Gore's church. Mrs. Evans of the Mason District Provident Association was a speaker that night, too, and some of the women involved in the strike were on the platform and some in the front seats and they stated their criticism of the rules under which they worked."[64]

Unquestionably, the militancy and significant leadership of the Black women was one of the unique features of this struggle.

After the third day of the strike, Funsten offered the workers a 33-1/3 percent increase in wages, which was roundly rejected.[65] He also indicated he would propose an increase for the white workers that would be beneficial to them.[66] When interviewed by the press, Funsten said, "When times were good, we passed a larger share of the earnings along to the workers; now that they are not, we have had to reduce their pay."[67] The St. Louis *Argus*, reflected on this complaint in one of its columns; "The plea of the company that any higher wages would cause the plant to operate at a loss is not in keeping with the present price of nut meat, which averages forty cents per pound. It would not take the mind of Einstein to calculate the vast amount of profit the producer of this commodity would receive at these wages."[68] In an earlier interview with the St. Louis *Post-Dispatch* Funsten had stated, "... Our company has not made a profit for more than two years and is not likely to earn anything until conditions improve materially."[69]

In our conversation with Hugh L. King, president of Funsten Nut Company — Division of Pet Milk, we were informed that the nut industry, because it was not a high cost item, was affected very little by the prevailing economic conditions of the depression. He also indicated that the rate of profit at that time was about 10%.[70] A few calculations indicate to us that the Funsten profit yearly must have been about $250,000.

Following their rejection of this Funsten offer and its subsequently being reported in the press, the women decided to demonstrate in front of city hall and solicit the assistance of the mayor. *Labor Unity* reported that fifteen hundred women, including some men, marched down to the city hall.[71] The St. Louis *Post-Dispatch* cited the figure of around four hundred and fifty.[72]

*Labor Unity* calculated that during the course of the strike, about one hundred women were arrested and taken to jail.[73] This figure seems to be a high estimate based on the newspaper reports. However, there were a number of arrests in connection with the strike. This appears to have increased the militancy of the women, who then physically prevented strikebreakers from entering the one plant where this was happening. Police brought strikebreakers to and from work in patrol wagons and taxis. After an attempt to convince the strikebreakers failed, the strike committee hand picked one hundred women — who let loose with bricks, bats and other objects against the scabs who were taking their jobs.[74] In her recollection of such occurrences and also explaining why she didn't join in, Mrs. Franklin said, "There were some fights. They were trying to keep some of them from going back in. One lady went in and she worked all day and her husband came that evening for her and they beat him terrible. He was trying to keep them from hurting his wife. None were hurt much in the fighting, a little knot in the head or bust of the skin. We just watched from the window of the restaurant across the street and went on home. I would know better what to do.... I'm not going out there to fight. 'Cause I do see they have to carry some to the hospital, some to jail. Ambulance was there. The biggest of them went to jail."[75]

While Mrs. Franklin stated that the police were there to keep order, the *Post-Dispatch* reported on May 18th that William Sentner, the union organizer, complained that the police were preventing peaceful picketing and that this could lead to trouble. The May 19th edition reported two arrests of strikers, as well as a police officer who suffered a dislocated knee in an attempt to avoid flying missiles.[76]

The *Daily Worker* reported, "Workers prevented the police from breaking up the picket lines by smashing two police cars and taxi cabs carrying strikebreakers."[77]

Referring to a "vicious attack ... made on the picket lines by police" a later edition reported the arrest of fifteen pickets including union organizer, Sentner.[78] Another offer of 75 cents per 25 lb. box of shelled nuts was made by Funsten and it also was rejected. On May 23rd the central strike committee met in an all day session with Funsten, his attorney and the Mayor's committee. An offer was tentatively agreed upon. This was brought back to the strikers, who voted unanimously to accept the offer of 90 cents for a 25 lb. box of unshelled nuts which, on the pound basis, was the equivalent of eight cents for halves and four cents for pieces. Other small companies also met the demand of eight and four.[79]

Fourteen hundred members joined the newly established eleven locals of the Food Workers Industrial Union.[80] Organization of locals began in East St. Louis, where Funsten employed nine hundred women workers.

Shop committees were elected and rules agreed upon as to how to check each member for a union card and dues payment before each could enter the shop. The duties of the shop committees included the handling of any grievances. A city central board of the union with representatives from each local union was established to meet every week and decide policy. Executive committees of each local were elected. Only one newspaper, the *Daily Worker*, reported in its May 29th edition of a meeting lasting up to midnight between the union and the Company which resulted in a reversal of a company decision to lay off one-third of the workers following the victorious strike.[81]

Several persons interviewed referred to subsequent strikes by the women, the cause of which seemed unclear to them. Mr. Shaw explained that "after the strike, some of the cheating (on the weight) continued and that was one of the things that there was some rebellion on after the union was recognized. There were some bitter complaints on that. There was some side strikes on that after the union was recognized. There was some discussions to organize the men to waylay these guys and beat the hell out of them when the women would point out who they were. The union itself was against that policy. They said the union leadership should go to protest openly rather than do a terroristic job." There was also rebellion against speed-up in production in order to make up for the loss incurred from the increase in wages.[82]

Among the people interviewed, Harry Baldwin indicated that the workers got the union, but it wasn't long after that the company started moving parts of its operation down south.[83]

There appear to be some indications that following the strike, some mechanization was instituted and that this was followed by layoffs.

Objecting to the layoffs and demanding reemployment, the union called for mass picketing. When seven hundred pickets surrounded the plant, police came along with wagons and arrested seventy-five pickets "without any cause." The strikers, who held a public trial with a workers' jury composed of nut pickers, clothing workers, miners and members of the AFL, found the company "in violation of the NRA pledge, misuse of NRA signs, deception of the public and attempt to further speed up the workers and cut down on the force."[84]

The move out of the city, technique of the runaway shop, combined with the arrests without cause indicate that the company and the city were anxious to cool the situation and avoid another eruption.

In July it was reported in the *Argus* that the Hoffman Bros. Nut Co. workers received an increase which, "corresponds with that adopted by the Funsten Nut Co. ... following a strike last May."[85]

Subsequently, a strike occurred at a Funsten plant on the east side which lasted for two weeks when three women refused to pay union dues of ten cents a week and management upheld their right not to pay. The union demanded that the workers pay their dues or stop working at the factory. When the women refused, the union ordered a suspension of work and the strike ensued. In reporting upon the incident, the St. Louis *Argus* said, "This union has caused the women to have shorter hours, more pay and better working conditions and it is believed by many of the workers that the management's upholding of the three women was in order to cause a walkout and break up the union. This wanton disregard has not helped the three women any and has caused hundreds of women to miss their regular pay-

37

checks and usual employment during the strike."[86] From the above incident, it would appear that the union did make an effort to safeguard the hard-won rights of the women. However, it is important to realize that all of this activity took place before the establishment of the National Labor Relations Board, NLRB.

With regard to the industry in general, expansion was reported as soon as September 25, 1933, at which time the following was reported in *St. Louis Business, 1931-1935:* "National Pecan Marketing Association ... formerly at Jackson, Mississippi, has leased three floors in the Tyler Warehouse and Cold Storage Building ... The Association ... employs ten persons at present ... fifteen persons will be employed November 1.... About $5,000 worth of machinery has been installed...." This group is the selling agency for a group of twenty local associations.[87]

# ROLE OF THE COMMUNIST PARTY

As indicated earlier, the strike originated with a Communist who first approached a few women workers at Funsten, who happened to be in his family, with the idea of organizing a union.

The Communist Party was in the leadership of the Trade Union Unity League, established in 1929, of which the Food Workers Industrial Union was an affiliate. The FWIU came into existence as a result of a split with the Amalgamated Food Workers in 1930. This Left-oriented group had its stronghold in New York, where it organized hundreds of small strikes. Its major problem was one of court injunctions issued to prevent union organization. In keeping with TUUL policy, it followed the principle of mass violation of injunctions and hundreds of its members were jailed. At its peak, it had a national membership of 10,000. The formation of the TUUL was dedicated to:

(1) The establishment of new unions where the AFL unions were decrepit or nonexistent.

(2) Commitment to continue to work within already existing unions.

(3) To unite the struggles of the unemployed with the employed.

Its essential commitment was to industrial unionism. In 1933 it began to merge into the AFL in an effort to support new elements emerging with the AFL, like the Committee on Industrial Organization under the leadership of John L. Lewis. This was predicated on the notion of building unity and in opposition to dualism. The merger was finally completed by the end of 1934.[88]

Prior to the Funsten strike, the FWIU had not existed in St. Louis.

The local leader of the Communist Party, Ralph Shaw, a former coal miner and subsequently an organizer for the steel union in the CIO, was involved from the outset in the initial stages of the organization of the women at Funsten. The representative of the Food Workers Industrial Union, William Sentner, who subsequently became its official organizer, and much later became a national director of organization for the CIO in this area, was a member of the leading body of the local Communist Party. Much of the party membership was involved in supportive activities relating to the Funsten strike. The demand of equal pay for equal work, and the involvement of the white workers in the leadership roles, despite their small numbers, was consonant with the philosophy of the Party to fight for Black-white unity, to fight for the rights and organization of Black workers, as well as for the rights of women. This arose from its theoretical doctrines, which at the same time viewed Black people both as an oppressed nation and as a critical segment of the working class. Also, its adherence to the Marxist concept of women in the Communist Manifesto: "The less the skill and exertion of strength implied in manual labor, the more is the labor of men superseded by that of women. Differences of age and sex have no longer any distinctive social validity for the working class. All are instruments of labor, more or less expensive to use, according to their age and sex."

In November 1931, in New York, the Food Workers Industrial Union had a convention, at which time it overhauled its constitution and adopted provisions for greater decentralization. It also established department for Negroes, women and young workers.[89]

41

# NATIONAL UNEMPLOYED COUNCIL

Another avenue through which Communist influence occurred in the strike was through the assistance and participation in various activities by members of the Unemployed Councils.

The National Unemployed Council was an organization established by the Communists under the slogans of "DON'T STARVE—FIGHT" and "WORK OR WAGES." A good deal of its national focus was based on efforts to get legislation passed for unemployment insurance at the expense of the government and the employers, established on the basis of the average wages of employed workers. It was organized into neighborhood, block and city councils on a non dues-paying basis. The major form of struggle was mass demonstration, but the Council also performed a social service function when it fought for relief in individual cases. Among its national demonstrations were National Unemployment Day held on February 25, 1931 with 400,000 demonstrators and again on February 4, 1932 with 500,000 participants.

However, its major emphasis was on local struggles, which sought to compel reluctant city authorities to grant relief to starving masses of unemployed workers. These local demonstrations generated a good deal of violence on the part of the police against the demonstrators.[90]

Compared to other large cities, St. Louis had a smaller Unemployed Council, with its neighborhood branches. Nevertheless it was very active and had considerable impact. In July 1932, a cutback of relief to 15,000 families plus a possible 8,000 more precipitated a variety of actions that led to the "July Riot." It was estimated that 15,000 demonstrators, many of whom were Black, participated. "Most of the opposition to the police came from Negroes who backed away from the gas, but threw bricks picked up from a wrecked building across the street..." "... in the summer of 1932,...the movement reached a... peak...it was Black unemployed workers, men and women, who played the leading and most fearless role." Black participation was disproportionately high in this movement compared to their percentage within the working class in the city. "... they appeared as both spokesmen and delegates repeatedly."[91] Some of the most able and effective organiz-

43

ers among these workers joined the Communist Party.

The Funsten strikers drew much of their support and leadership from the Communist Party and from the communist-led Unemployed Councils.

## Attitude of the Workers Toward the Communist Role

Despite the many attacks by Funsten, his attorney, Lashley, the mayor and others upon the communist leadership and influence, the evidence indicates that the striking women were not adversely affected. In fact, when an attempt was made to oust William Sentner from the negotiations with the mayor, his appointed committee and Funsten, the women made their position quite clear by "insisting" that he be part of the negotiating committee as their union representative, and they would remain only so long as he participated.[92] Most of the general strike committee meetings were held at the Communist Party headquarters and it was there that the mayor came to address the workers — exhorting them to accept the offer, which he explained to them, and which ended in victory.

# ROLE OF THE URBAN LEAGUE

In an interview with Mrs. Buckner, who was employed by the League at that time, she recalled that, "The League did not take an active part in this strike. Our problem was to replace the women who were spending their time picking nuts. The Negro women working in these storefronts ... many of them had open sores on their arms and their hands — no health requirements were enforced — and for that reason the League wasn't interested in furthering their cause. But we did have several meetings out in the community about that." It should be noted, however, that John Clark, the League's executive secretary, was appointed to the Mayor's investigating committee. In looking through Mr. Clark's papers, I did note a general concern on the part of the League about Communist influence on Black people during that period. The League considered itself a social service agency, with much of its funding from local businesses.

Prior to the strike there were community groups including the Urban League who had knowledge of the working conditions of the nut workers, but appear to have ignored them. one such reference is contained in an editorial by Rabbi Isserman (pp. 51-2).* Additional corroborating evidence can be noted in an article by Bill Gebert in the theoretical journal of the Communist Party, *The Communist*. Gebert wrote, "These conditions among Negro women in St. Louis have existed for years. The Urban League and all other Negro organizations never paid any attention to this miserable indescribable slavery...."[93]

* Also Appendix III

# ROLE OF THE CITY GOVERNMENT

The election of Mayor Bernard Dickman in 1932 was a historic event. He was the first Democratic mayor of St. Louis to be elected in 24 years. He was swept into office with the election of President Franklin D. Roosevelt and the New Deal, and this was partially accounted for because, for the first time, Black voters had voted for a Democratic ticket.[94]

The Funsten strike occurred shortly after he took office. When the first offer of an increase made by Funsten was turned down by the strikers as inadequate, the central strike committee decided to visit Mayor Dickman and ask his assistance in arbitrating the strike. In addition, because 60% of the women were receiving aid from the Provident Association, they planned a demonstration at city hall to dramatize their plight. When the delegation of three Black and two white women together with William Sentner arrived at City Hall, the mayor was not there and they conferred with the Associate City Counselors who agreed to pass their request on to the Mayor. A few days later, a large crowd of women strikers marched to city hall from strike headquarters. The mayor came out to address the women, tell-

47

ing them that while he favored "just pay," he did not believe that the strike was a municipal matter, but he agreed to meet with a small committee.[95]

Subsequently, he appointed a citizen's committee to investigate the complaint concerning low wages. The committee included Rabbi Ferdinand Isserman of Temple Israel, the Rev. William Markoe of St. Elizabeth's Catholic Church, John T. Clark, Executive Secretary of the Urban League, O. O. Morris of Negro Y.M.C.A., William H. Parker, Negro Attorney, Emmett Canty, Chief Parole officer and Joseph L. McLemore, Negro Attorney with the Legal Aid Bureau of the city. The Mayor stated that the purpose of the committee was not as arbitrators whose findings must by accepted, but they were to listen to both sides of the story and attempt to bring about an agreement.

According to the then Assistant City Counselor David Grant, the mayor appointed the committee to get the heat off and stymie the communists who were making great headway with these issues."[96] At a meeting Grant attended with the mayor's committee, Funsten stated that he didn't know whether Mr. Lashley was representing Funsten or not. Whereupon Lashley, seated next to Grant, commented under his breath, "I'm representing myself." By way of further explanation, it was pointed

48

out to the author that at this initial meeting it was clear that it was extremely difficult to uphold the hand of a sweatshop.

Subsequently, the mayor called the citizen's committee, the strikers and the Funsten representatives together in a meeting which lasted all day and finally resulted in the offer that the strikers accepted at a general meeting. The mayor accompanied the strike committee to its headquarters, which was the headquarters of the Communist Party, and urged the strikers to accept the proposed offer. With the mayor was the Black Assistant City Counselor David Grant who thanked the Communists for alleviating the miserable conditions under which his people had labored.

Following the settlement of the Funsten strike, the mayor appointed Attorney Parker, at the suggestion of David Grant, as a building inspector. This gave him easy access to investigate other sweatshops in the city. Attorney Parker made his report on working conditions directly to the mayor, who then called in the management of these shops and suggested that they rectify these conditions if they did not want a repetition of the events that had occurred at the Funsten factory. The general community reaction to the mayor's role was positive, except for the communists, who labeled it demagogic.

# THE PROVIDENT ASSOCIATION

While the Provident Association had been for many years a private charitable agency which did on occasion give assistance, it only did so in conjunction with therapy. During the depression it brought in Black social workers. Mrs. Elmer Moisee said that during this period the agency found, with the enormous numbers of unemployed and starving people, that these people would agree to anything in order to get assistance.[97]

In 1930 it became an affiliate agent of the Citizen's Committee on Relief for which it administered public funds.[98] Thus, when the strikers went to the city for aid, it was because the Provident Association was providing assistance as an agency acting on behalf of the city, administering and distributing city funds. It was this situation which prompted the union organizer to assert that the city was, therefore, subsidizing the Funsten company.

# COMMUNITY REACTION

As we indicated earlier, the strikers did take their plight to various community groups to arouse support for their struggle. One such group was the St. Louis Commission for Social Justice, composed of clergy and university professors.

Rabbi Isserman, a member of the mayor's appointed Citizen's Committee, was also a member of the Commission. Among several editorials that Rabbi Isserman wrote regarding the Funsten strike, he said the following: "... employers in local nut factories who were underpaying their workers had attempted to discredit their strike by ascribing it to communist agitation. We suggested ... these employers were ... seeking to confuse the real issues by injecting communism. We were in error.... The nut-pickers' strike was not inspired by Communists but it was led by Communists. It was inspired by a wage scale which was unAmerican, and which did not make possible even the barest subsistence for the workers. If it had not been for the Communist leaders, this tragic condition would not have been brought to light. The Urban

League and other organizations interested in colored people were familiar with this situation.... No doubt that their strike was justified. Not propaganda makes Communism but injustice on the part of the community or on the part of individuals in the community."

In another editorial discussing juvenile delinquency, Rabbi Isserman had this to say. "One of the striking nut-pickers informed the Mayor's committee that her baby boy, eleven years of age, was at Bellefontaine, sent there because he had stolen. The mother earned $3.00 a week with which she was compelled to maintain herself and three children. The boy went out gathering kindling wood which he sold and purchased the things that he should have had and that his mother ... could not give him. The boy stole some wood and sold it. Now he is at Bellefontaine. He ran afoul of the law because his mother was the victim of sweat-shop methods. If the income of his family had been adequate, that boy today would be a respectable member of society."[99] (See appendix III and IV.)

# NEWSPAPER COMMENTARY

The strike did, indeed, receive extensive coverage in the press. It is interesting to note that the local newspapers, including the *Post Dispatch*, reported the practice of discrimination at the Funsten factory regarding the differential in wages between Black and white nutpickers. It was, however, only the St. Louis *Argus*, the local Black newspaper which decried this practice. In one of its editorials, the *Argus* remarked that the maintenance of this practice was evidence of the difficulties confronting Black workers in industry. Still further it noted that despite the wage differential, the company sold its product for the same price, thus leading the editor to conclude, "It looked to us like 'profiteering' off the Negro worker. Their (i.e. Communist Party) insistence on the same pay for the same class of work among the workers, both white and Black, can't but strike a popular cord in the minds of the colored people."[100] (See Appendix — editorials.)

It is significant that the *Post* did write, in addition to its coverage of the strike, two editorials on this local conflict. It's first editorial called for uniform minimum wage laws to offset wage slashing, sweatshop conditions and starvation wages, as well as urging the consumer to demonstrate a willingness to pay higher prices for nut products in order to insure the workers a living wage. In a subsequent editorial, it commented on the significance of the strike for future historians who would no doubt analyze the event in the context of the confused economics of that period. In a lamenting tone it went on to say that this "still unborn" historian would say that, while the victory of a 100 percent increase was a high ratio, he would, no doubt, conclude that it reflected "that much remained to be done in May, 1933, before labor's share in industry rose to the level where it could keep business alive by its role in mass buying power."[101] (See Appendix — editorials.)

## STATE REVERBERATION

In discussing the effects of the strike on workers organized into the American Federation of Labor, one article commented that its impact was reflected on the floor of the state convention. Gebert says, "At the convention of the Missouri State Federation of Labor ... rank and file delegates raised the question of the nut pickers' strike, demanding that the A.F. of L. change its policy of conducting strike struggles and adopt the policy developed by the nut pickers. The bourgeois press was so alarmed by the sympathy shown by the rank and file delegates at the State Convention, that they spoke of a 'split' in the A.F. of L."[102] A limited investigation by the author could not find any further corroborating evidence in the proceedings of the State Convention held in May, 1934 at Joplin. But verbatim discussions at conventions are not usually recorded.

However, on page 14 of the proceedings, there is a statement headed "Notable Achievements of the Labor Movement of the Past Year." It states. "It is very significant that strikes and controversies have indeed been very few and those that have occurred of any moment have been brought on by the stubborn refusal of anti-union employers to allow their employees to organize a union of their choice in accordance with the provisions of Section 7(a) of the National Recovery Act. The fine discipline that has been maintained by the labor movement during these trying times is an everlasting credit to the intelligent statesmanship and patriotism of the members of the great labor movement and its leaders."[103]

What does seem to be clear is that the AFL did not adopt this policy and thus, one might conclude, laid the basis for the emergence of the CIO. It would seem that individual members of the AFL were positively affected by the Funsten strike but that this was not true of the official organization.

# CONCLUSION

From the outset, the nutpickers' strike was an outgrowth of the conditions existing during that time. More specifically, it can be classified as a part of the movements which refused to succumb to those conditions and, thereby, acted as a mechanism through which hopelessness was negated by hope. In following closely the sequence of events, one would have to say that the strike was an outgrowth of the activity of the Unemployed Councils in St. Louis.

Despite the expressed interest in organizing women workers on the part of those who were responsible for initiating this struggle, we would conclude that the organization of the Funsten workers was primarily motivated by the general concept of industrial unionism with its specific emphasis on organizing the unorganized — particularly, the unskilled and the semi-skilled. Insofar as women happened, not by accident, to predominate in these categories, it can be inferred that the strike did positively fulfill commitment to this doctrine. The same can be concluded with regard to the organization of Black workers.

The Funsten Nutpickers' Strike was indeed historic. When one views it in the context of the times, one is impressed with its audacious quality. In the midst of the depression, these women workers had the daring to ask for an increase in wages. In a totally jimcrow setting, these Black women workers had the courage to challenge an important corporate enterprise as well as the power structure of the city government. In an era when wage differentials were an accepted way of life, the Funsten nutpickers demanded equal pay for equal work for Black and white workers. One may well wonder how they convinced the white women to accept this notion. The reality of the situation was that wages for Black and white women were incredibly low despite the differential. Nevertheless, it is to the credit of the leadership of this strike that it had the commitment and the imagination to establish this issue as one of its demands. Finally, it is important to record the unique feature of this struggle in the role of the Black women as the pivotal force that propelled it forward to a successful conclusion.

We can ponder whether the demise of the TUUL into the CIO, in an effort to build the latter, which concentrated on organizing workers in basic industrial production, did

58

not have an adverse effect on the organization of women. The immediate result of the Funsten Strike in St. Louis was that it acted as a catalyst for the clothing workers strike that developed in August 1933. When questioned on this, Ralph Shaw responded by saying, "This initial example by the most oppressed nut workers had a tremendous effect in St. Louis in bringing forward the clothing workers and ladies' garment union strike after the NRA was passed. Some of our people from the Food Union spoke and were greeted at some of their strike meetings. There was a tremendous feeling of solidarity. This is what dramatized all of the oppressed's feeling. This strike brought us close to Michaelson (a leader of the Amalgamated Clothing Workers union locally) and the clothing workers. Immediately after our strike, I remember Michaelson calling me and saying 'we're gonna walk out.' The women don't want any of that - - - - anymore. The Ladies Garment Union tripled its membership as a result of this strike. The feeling among the CIO leaders was that we had just set the stage for the CIO."[104]

Reports in the *Post Dispatch* indicate that on August 10, 1933 at a meeting of the International Ladies Garment Workers Union,

59

where 1400 workers were present, women operators agreed to seek union recognition. Present and extending greetings to that meeting was the leadership of the Amalgamated Clothing Workers Union from Chicago. Also present was W. Brandt, Acting Secretary of the Central Trades and Labor Union, AFL. Shortly thereafter, the garment workers went out on strike. On August 11, the Amalgamated Clothing Workers threatened a strike. Later in August, they joined with the ILGWU in what became an industry-wide strike that lasted six months.

On August 9, 1933 the *Post* reported that 500 out of 7,000 Laundry Workers joined the newly organized Laundry Workers Union; 80% of these workers were women, nearly half were Black. The immediate cause of unionization was the complaint of starvation wages.

Finally on August 13, 1933 the *Post* reported that the Office Workers Union, following an extended period of being dormant, would hold a mass meeting.

There is no doubt that the result of these struggles was the organization of large numbers of women, Black and white, into trade unions.

Some of the women active in the nutpickers' strike were involved at a later date in integrating the work force of the small arms plant on Goodfellow Ave. and were the core that helped organize all the small arms plants into the United Electrical and Radio Workers of America, an affiliate of the CIO.[104]

Insofar as the CIO followed the same policy of the TUUL with regard to industrial unionism and the organization of the unskilled and semi-skilled, it did organize larger numbers of women and Black workers into its ranks.[105]

# NOTES

1. Arthur M. Schlesinger, *New Viewpoints in American History*, New York, MacMillan Co., 1922
2. W.E.B. DuBois, Preface to Herbert Aptheker, ed., *A Documentary History of the Negro People in the United States*, New York, Citadel Press, 1951
3. *Women at Work*, U.S. Department of Labor, Women's Bureau, 1933
4. Grace Hutchins, *Women Who Work*, New York, International Publishers, 1934
5. *Ibid.*
6. *Ibid.*
7. *Ibid.*
8. *Annual Report*, Missouri Department of Labor Statistics, 1929-1931
9. Federal Census, Metropolitan St. Louis by Tracts, 1930
10. *Ibid.*
11. Joseph Borus, "Negro Standard of Living in St. Louis in 1932," Thesis, June 1933
12. *Women at Work*, 1933
13. Charles Prince, *The Social and Economic Conditions of Garment Workers in St. Louis*, Thesis; June 1932
14. Amanda Hargis, Commissioner, *1931 Report*, State Department of Labor and Inspections
15. "A Century of Industrial Change," *Women at Work*, U.S. Department of Labor, Women's Bureau, 1933
16. Prince, *Garment Workers*, June 1932
17. *Ibid.*
18. *Women at Work*, 1933
19. Herbert Hill, "The Racial Practices of Organized Labor," Julius Jacobson. ed., *The Negro and the American Labor Movement*, Garden City, New York, Anchor Books, Doubleday & Co., 1968
20. Interview with Mrs. Elmer Moisee, Retired Social Worker, Provident Association
21. Letter from Antonia Sentner, wife of deceased union organizer, William Sentner
22. *Century of Change*, U.S. Department of Labor, Women's Bureau, 1933

23. The Papers of John Clark, formerly Executive Secretary, Urban League of St. Louis, 1933, Washington University Archives

24. Mrs. J. Buckner, Retired Field Representative and Placement Secretarys Urban League of St. Louis, 1933, as related in an interview

25. Gould's *St. Louis Red Blue Book*, St, Louis, Mo., Polk-Gould Directory Co., 1928

26. Howard S.F. Randolph, *Ancestors and Descendants of Col. David Funsten and His Wife Susan Everard Meade*, New York, H.F. Durand, 1926

27. *Book of St. Louisans*, St. Louis Mo., St. Louis Republic, 1906, 1912

28. From the files of the Funsten Nut Co. as looked up and reported by the secretary employed there.

29. Ralph Shaw, "St. Louis' Biggest Strike," *Labor Unity*, Publication of the TUUL, August 1933; St. Louis *Post Dispatch*, May 18, 1933; Interviews with Ralph Shaw and Ed Shannon

30. Conversation with Hugh L. King, President, Funsten Nut Co.— Division of Pet Milk

31. *Ibid.*

32. As recalled in an interview with Mary Franklin and Lottie Johnson

33. As recalled in interviews with Nora Diamond and Evelina Ford

34. Interview with Evelina Ford

35. As recalled in an interview with David Grant, former Assistant City Counselor, City of St. Louis

36. St. Louis *Post Dispatch,* May 18, 1933

37. Shaw, *Labor Unity*, August, 1933

38. Interview with Mrs. Elmer Moisee

39. As recalled in an interview with Mrs. Josie Moore

40. Interview with Mrs. J. Buckner

41. Shaw, *Labor Unity*, August, 1933

42. St. Louis *Star Times*, May 24, 1933

43. St. Louis *Post Dispatch*, May 21, 1933 / *Daily Worker*, June 1, 1933

44. Shaw, *Labor Unity*, August, 1933

45. St, Louis *Argus*, May 26, 1933, Vol. 22 #6

46. Interviews with Mrs. Buckner and Mr. Shaw

47. Interview with Mrs. Buckner

48. Bill Gebert, "The St. Louis Strike and the Chicago Needle Trade Strike," *The Communist*, Vol. XII, No. 8, August, 1933; interview with Ralph Shaw, former leader, Communist Party of St. Louis

49. Shaw, *Labor Unity*, August 1933, plus interview with Mr. Shaw

50. Interview with Mary Franklin
51. Shaw, *Labor Unity*, August, 1933
52. Shaw, *Labor Unity*, August, 1933
53. Interview with Nora Diamond
54. St. Louis *Argus*, May 19, 1933, Vol. #5
55. St. Louis *Post Dispatch*, May 17, 1933
56. Gebert, *Daily World*, June 1, 1933
57. Interview with Shaw
58. St. Louis *Star Times*, May 24, 1933
59. St. Louis *Post Dispatch*, May 18, 1933
60. St. Louis *Post Dispatch*, May 23, 1933
61. *Ibid.*
62. Interview with Shaw
63. St. Louis *Post Dispatch*, May 19, 1933
64. Interview with Mrs. Buckner
65. St. Louis *Post Dispatch*, May 19, 1933; Shaw, *Labor Unity*, August, 1933
66. St. Louis *Post Dispatch*, May 16, 1933
67. St. Louis *Post Dispatch*, May 18, 1933
68. St. Louis *Argus*, May 26, 1933, Vol. 22 #6
69. St. Louis *Post Dispatch*, May, 16, 1933
70. Conversation with Hugh L. King
71. Shaw, *Labor Unity*, August, 1933
72. St. Louis *Post Dispatch*, May 23, 1933
73. Shaw, *Labor Unity*, August, 1933
74. *Ibid.*
75. Interview with Mrs. Franklin
76. St. Louis *Post Dispatch*, May 18, 1933 and May 19, 1933
77. *Daily Worker*, May 22, 1933
78. *Daily Worker*, May 23, 1933
79. St. Louis *Post Dispatch*, May 24, 1933; Shaw, *Labor Unity*, August, 1933
80. *Daily Worker*, May 29, 1933
81. *Ibid.*
82. Interview with Shaw
83. As recalled in an interview with Huray Baldwin
84. St. Louis *Argus*, October 13, 1933
85. St. Louis *Argus*, July 21, 1933
86. St. Louis *Argus*, March 30, 1934
87. *St. Louis Business* 1931-1935, September 25, 1933
88. William Z. Foster, *From Bryan to Stalin*, New York, International Publishers, 1937
89. *The American Labor Yearbook*, Rand School Press, 1932

90. Foster, *From Bryan to Stalin*, 1937, p. 228. Foster also cites the Dec. 7, 1931 National Hunger March that brought 1800 delegates to Washihgton and a second one, Dec. 6, 1932, with 3000 delegates

91. St. Louis *Post Dispatch* and Dennis Brunn, unpublished thesis on Black workers in the 1930s in the St. Louis labor movement

92. St. Louis *Post Dispatch*, May 23, 1933; Gebert, *The Communist*, August, 1933

93. Gebert, *The Communist*, August, 1933

94. Interview with David Grant

95. St. Louis *Post Dispatch*, May 23, 1933

96. Interview with David Grant

97. Interview with Mrs. Elmer Moisee

98. A. Vanek, "St. Louis Provident Association 1931-1935," Thesis, June 1938

99. From the papers of Rabbi Ferdinand Isserman, Editorial from *The Modern View*, St. Louis, Mo., Vol. 66 #15, Thursday, May 25, 1933, American Jewish Archives, Hebrew Union College

100. St. Louis *Argus*, May 26, 1933, Vol. 22 #6

101. St. Louis *Post Dispatch*, editorials, May 20, 1933 and May 26, 1933

102. Gebert, *The Communist*, August, 1933

103. Proceedings of the State Convention of the Missouri State, American Federation of Labor, May, 1934, Joplin

104. Shaw Interview

105. Letter from Antonia Sentner

# Appendix I

# GIRLS
## Both White AND Negro

Last Saturday night there was a meeting of girls from the Funsten Nut factories at 16th and Morgan and 4200 Easton, called by the Food Workers Industrial Union Locals of both factories.

At this meeting we decided that we could no longer bear our starvation wages of from -- $1.50 to $3.00 a week for 50 hours of hard work. ~~They decided that the girls and works~~ We decided that we would make one final demand for an answer to our request for a wage of 10 for halves and 4 for pieces. If this would not be granted to us, we would strike and force the boss to give it to us.

Girls: Stand ready! We will let you know if it is necessary to come out with us and go to the main office and place out demands. We will give you a signal for walkout. Stand ready. We cannot let the boss starve us any longer!

Food Workers Industrial Union
Easton Ave. Local
16th- Morgan Local

## NOTICE

Tonight at 1243 N. Garrison, at 8 P.M. there will be held a meeting called by the union. Come and hear what has been done and what we must do further. Let us organize ourselves into a union that will help us get better wages and conditions and keep them when we do get them.

1243 N. GARRISON.        TONIGHT        8 P.M.

# STICK TOGETHER
## DEMAND
# 10 AND 4

# TO THE
# WORKERS OF ST. LOUIS!

SUPPORT The Striking Nut Pickers of St Louis

ORGANIZE Relief Committees in Shops, Trade Unions, and in your neighborhoods

ORGANIZE Committees in the Factories and prepare for your own strike for increased wages and shorter working hours

**COMRADES AND BROTHERS:**

ELEVEN HUNDRED Negro and White women of the Funston Nut Factories are on strike. Sixty-five Negro women of the American Nut Manufacturing Company joined these underpaid workers in strike this morning. Workers in other nut factories are preparing to join the strike.

THE STRIKERS demand an increase in wages to 10c for halves and 4c for pieces. Their present rates average only $1.80 a week, and only the most skilled workers earn as much as $3.00 a week. These girls deserve and demand an increase so that they can live and eat and pay rent and bills.

THIS STRIKE of the White and Negro women of the nut Factories against sweatshop conditions and starvation wages must be supported by every worker in St. Louis. It is your strike, as well as their own. This strike can be won with your support. Strikers have organized a Food Workers' Industrial Union—affiliated with the Trade Union Unity League.

WORKERS IN EVERY SHOP, Workers who are members of the A. F. L and Railroad Brotherhoods, organize at once Relief Committees in your shops, in your Union, so that hunger will not drive these women back to slavery conditions and starvation wages. Send all contributions and food, money, clothing to The Striker's Relief Committee, 1243 N. Garrison Ave., St. Louis.

POLICE are attempting to break up mass picket lines and they arrest the picketers. Fellow workers, you must join the picket lines to strengthen this strike.

WORKERS IN THE SHOPS, you are starving while working. Your wages have been cut to the bone; working conditions have steadily become worse. You work long hours under the nerve-racking speed-up. You must follow the steps of these nut pickers; you must organize yourselves, and strike! Call a meeting of the workers in your factory: discuss the conditions, formulate demands, and prepare to strike, like these workers, against oppressive conditions.

UNEMPLOYED WORKERS—men and women, Negro and White—your task is to support every one of these strike strugglers; their struggle is your struggle. Join the picket lines at once. Organize to serve in the Unemployed Council, so you together with workers in the shops can fight against these same bosses—demand adequate cash relief and Unemployment Insurance at the rightful expense of the bosses and the Government.

NEGRO AND WHITE WORKERS, bosses are always throwing a wedge between us. The bosses' gain lies in our division. The strength of the working class and their victory depend upon the unity of the Negro and the White in common struggle.

THE CITY GOVERNMENT, headed by Mayor Dickmann and his police, are with the bosses They serve the bosses' interest. But when we unite our forces nothing can stop us from achieving our aims.

TRADE UNION UNITY LEAGUE OF ST. LOUIS, under whose leadership nut pickers are striking, call upon the workers of St. Louis to come out in united action, to organize and strike for increase of wages, for shortened working hours; and to support the strike of these oppressed nut pickers.

CITY COUNCIL TRADE UNION UNITY I
1243 NORTH GARRIF

# Appendix III

*This editorial reproduced with the permission of American Jewish Archives, Cincinnati Campus of the Hebrew Union College–Jewish Institute of Religion.*

| Volume 66 | 5693—THURSDAY, MAY 25—1933 | Number 15 |

## EDITORIAL

*All editorials, unless denoted otherwise, are written by Rabbi Ferdinand M. Isserman and are signed F. M. I.*

### THE MORAL OF THE NUT-PICKERS' STRIKE

In our editorial of last week about breeding Communists, we suggested that the employers in local nut factories who were underpaying their workers had attempted to discredit their strike by describing it to Communist agitation. We then suggested that these employers were thereby seeking to confuse the real issues by injecting Communism. We were in error in our statement. The nut-pickers' strike was not inspired by Communists but it was led by Communists. It was inspired by a wage scale which was un-American, and which did not make possible even the barest subsistence for the workers. If it had not been for Communist leaders this tragic condition would not have been brought to light. The Urban League and other organizations interested in colored people were familiar with this situation. They lacked, however, the vigorous leadership to bring this condition to light. It is indeed a pity that in our city the only group prepared to speak for eight hundred exploited negro workers were members of the Communist party. While this strike was on and these hundreds of people and their dependents were foodless, their Communist leaders again provided them with food. Some of the workers informed us that they ate better food during this strike than they could afford to eat when they were earning $2.00 or $3.00 a week for forty-four hours of work. We visited the hall wherein they were fed and saw the fare they regarded as so excellent. It consisted of a platter of rice, a small piece of meat and a few crusts of bread. It was pathetic to observe how carefully some of them clutched a few extra crusts of bread which was perhaps to be their breakfast the next day. These strikers could not have been fed through the charitable agencies. No one doubts that their strike was justified. It was so justified that the Mayor of our city and the City Counsellor, as well as a number of other citizens, all of them busy men, gave up several days of their time to adjust the situation.

What will the effect of this strike be upon these thousand workers? They will feel indebted to the Communist party for its leadership. They may understand not one iota of the Communist platform or philosophy but they do understand that it rescued them from a degrading level of living. Not propaganda makes Communism, but injustice on the part of the community or on the part of individuals in the community. When the New Deal becomes evident and work and food and recreation is again available for the masses of the American people, then the red bogey of revolution will cease to be upon the horizon.

In stating their case the employers pointed out that they are compelled to compete with the cheap labor of some of our southern states where we are informed that a system almost equivalent to peonage exists. They added that if compelled to pay much higher wages they will take their industry from St. Louis. We appreciate the importance of industries to St. Louis, to its economic welfare and to its cultural and spiritual growth. But industries which degrade the level of living, which are compelled to pay outrageous wages, whose workers need assistance from the charities, are liabilities and not assets, spiritual liabilities as well as economic liabilities. St. Louis wants industries only in order that its residents may be able to live decently. Industries which make indecent living imperative ought to be informed that they are not wanted. The citizens of our community do not want to introduce in their midst the level of living which unfortunately disgraces some of the industrial areas of a few of the southern states.

—F. M. I.

# Appendix V

**Editorial**
St. Louis *Post Dispatch* 5/20/33
NUT PICKERS ON STRIKE

The strike of 500 women nut pickers in a local nut packing company is an instance right at home of an industrial condition that is attracting alarmed attention over the country. Two years ago, these Negro women earned $15 or $16 a week. Now, after a series of pay cuts, their average wage is only $1.80, and the most skilled get only $3. for a 52-hour week. This is far short of a living wage, and their employer, Eugene M. Funsten, frankly admits as much. He explains, however, that the industry is highly competitive, and that his firm must meet the prices of Southern concerns, which pay even lower wages. He has offered the strikers a pay increase of 33 1/3 per cent, expressing a hope that rising commodity prices will justify it.

The situation here shows how wage slashing has got out of hand in many industries, forcing sweatshop conditions and starvation wages on workers whose employers must meet their rivals' cuts or go out of business. This condition, to which attention has lately been drawn by Mr. Roosevelt, Secretary Perkins and a host of others, is the cause of the movement for minimum wage laws, such as New York State recently adopted, and the provision for "codes of fair competition" in the administration's bill for regulation of industry.

Has the public realized what a cost in human suffering is imposed by much of the "bargain" merchandise now on sale? In this instance, consumers of the nut products in which these women's cheap labor figures should be willing to pay higher prices if it will mean a living wage to the workers. But a uniform code of minimum wage laws and trade practices is the best solution offered to date for the vicious spiral of deflated wage scales.


**Editorial**
*Post-Dispatch*, 5/26/33
LOOKING BACK ON A STRIKE

Some future social historian, writing on the country's plight in 1933, may well view as a significant phenomenon of our times that 1200 adult woman workers in St. Louis went on strike against a wage scale of 50 cents and less a day, and won terms that were expected to double their pay. There will follow in his treatise a table of contemporary living costs, with a comment on the topsy-turvy economics of the period, that seemingly expected business to continue while consumers at the bottom of the labor scale, such as this group of nut pickers, earned too little to supply their own needs.

This still unborn historian also presumably will note that, while a 100 per cent increase was high in ratio, it scarcely made these workers important figures in buying power. In conclusion, he will sadly reflect, while conceding that the nut pickers' situation was an aggravated example of the epoch's wage-slashing and sweat shop conditions, that much remained to be done in May, 1933, before labor's share in industry rose to the level where it could keep business alive by its role in mass buying power.

# Appendix VI

**Editorial**
*St. Louis Argus*, 5/26/33
NUT PICKERS STRIKE

The disclosure of discrimination at the Funsten factory on prices paid for nut picking between white and colored workers furnishes quite a deal of food for thought. It shows the hard road which the colored worker has to travel in many of the industries which employ both white and colored.

The management of the Funsten factory admitted that it paid the white workers about one-third more for the same type of work, yet the management received the same price for the goods for which it paid the colored workers less.

It looked to us like "profiteering" off the Negro worker. With a little deeper thought on the matter, it may be that the management was profiteering off the white workers, but the strike has brought this condition to light, and according to the terms of the settlement, both white and colored workers will receive the same pay for the same class of work done.

Thus, the International Labor Defense and the Communist party have to their credit an expose, the results of which will mean much to the humble colored workers of the City. Their insistence on the same pay for the same class of work among the workers, both white and black, can't but strike a popular cord in the minds of the colored people.

CONFIDENTIALLY, if such an investigation was carried to the City Hall, it might reveal the same situation as was found in the nut factory— See.


Today and Yesterday, by Floyd J. Collins — *Argus*, 5/26/33
THE NUT PICKERS' STRIKE

The request of President Roosevelt to employers to refrain from their present practice of taking advantage of prevailing economic conditions and pay their employees a living wage was completely ignored by the R. E. Funsten Company. As a result 750 women whose pay for an average 40 hours was less than enough to meet the needs of the human body in keeping with standards of American living, 20 hours spent in leisure declared a strike. This effort of these poorly paid women is having a far reaching effect on the present scale of wages paid the laboring class and will do more to bring about the enactment of laws similar to the one recently passed by the New York legislature which will prohibit the paying of "starvation wages."

The plea of the company that any higher wages would cause the plant to operate at a loss is not in keeping with the present price of nut meat which averages forty cents per pound. It would not take the mind of Einstein to calculate the vast amount of profit the producer of this commodity would receive at these wages.

Regardless of the fact that Communist propaganda instigated this strike, these Negro women should be revered for their loyalty to a just cause.